THE EFFECT OF NETWORKING & CONNECTEDNESS

BUILDING STRATEGIC ALLIANCES FOR WOMEN

DR. MINAKSHI BANSAL

DEDICATION

To the women who dare to dream, who challenge the status quo, and who lift each other up. May your connections be your strength, your collaborations your fuel, and your collective impact your legacy.

Contents

Prayer ix

About The Author xi

Preface xv

1. Beyond The Business Card: Redefining Networking For Women 1

Part 1

2. The Power Of Connection: Unlocking The Potential Of Women's Networks 7

Part 2

3. Building Bridges: Creating Strategic Alliances For Mutual Success 13

Part 3

4. Navigating The Landscape: Women In Networking And Leadership 19

Part 4

5. Authenticity In Action: Cultivating Meaningful Professional Relationships 25

Part 5

6. The Art Of Conversation: Mastering The Skills Of Effective Networking 31

Part 6

7. Mentorship Matters: Empowering Women Through Guidance And Support 37

Part 7

8. Breaking Barriers: Overcoming Challenges In Building Alliances 43

Contents

Part 8

   9. Leveraging Technology: Expanding Your Network In The   49
      Digital Age

Part 9

   10. Finding Your Tribe: Building Community And Connection   55

Part 10

   11. Amplifying Your Voice: Sharing Your Expertise And Insights 61

Part 11

   12. Collaboration Over Competition: Embracing The Power Of   67
      Shared Success

Part 12

   13. From Networking To Net-Weaving: Creating A Strong Support 73
      System

Part 13

   14. Celebrating Success: Recognizing Achievements And   79
      Building Momentum

Part 14

   15. Paying It Forward: Supporting The Next Generation Of   85
      Women Leaders

Part 15

   16. Building A Legacy: The Lasting Impact Of Strategic Alliances 91

Part 16

   17. Thriving Together: The Power Of Collective Action   97

Part 17

   18. Networking For Social Impact: Creating Change Through   103
      Connection

Contents

Part 18

19. Cultivating Confidence: Stepping Into Your Power As A   109
    Networker"

Part 19

20. The Ripple Effect: Transforming Your Life And Career   115
    Through Networking

Part 20

21. SUMMARY   121

Citation and References   125

Other Books of the Author   127

CONTACT   133

Prayer

"Om Bhadram Karnebhih Shrinuyama Devah

Bhadram Pashyemakshabhiryajatrah

Sthirairangais Tushtuvamsastanubhih

Vyashema Devahitam Yadayuh

Svasti Na Indro Vriddhashravah

Svasti Nah Pusha Vishwavedah

Svasti Nastarkshyo Arishtanemih

Svasti No Brihaspatir Dadhatu

Om Shantih Shantih Shantih"

This mantra is a prayer for universal well-being, invoking the blessings of various deities for protection, health, and happiness. It emphasizes the importance of experiencing the auspicious through all senses and living a life aligned with divine purpose. The repetition of "Shantih" at the end signifies a deep desire for peace in the individual, the environment, and the universe at large. This mantra is often recited as a prayer for peace, prosperity, and the physical and spiritual well-being of all beings.

ᐳᐳᐳ

About The Author

This book represents the culmination of extensive research and meticulous analysis, incorporating a diverse range of sources, including numerous books, scholarly studies, and personal experiences. Additionally, I have scoured various websites to gather relevant information and data essential for the compilation of this work. I have taken every precaution to ensure the accuracy of the information presented and have diligently cited all sources to acknowledge their contributions.

From her earliest days, Minakshi was distinguished by an insatiable appetite for reading. Her literary universe was inhabited by characters and narratives that spanned ethical tales, motivational and inspirational stories, and the mythic parables imbued with life lessons. This voracious reading habit was not merely for personal edification but was driven by a desire to distill and disseminate the essence of these narratives to foster the development of students and peers alike. She was particularly captivated by the lives and teachings of historical figures and spiritual leaders such as Adi Shankaracharya, Swami Vivekananda, Dr. APJ Abdul Kalam, Mahamana Pandit Madan Mohan Malviya, Mahatma Gandhi, Sardar Vallabhai Patel, and Vinoba Bhave, among others. Their philosophies and life stories fueled her ambition to embody their ideals of resilience, selflessness, and relentless pursuit of knowledge.

Dr. Minakshi's academic and practical engagement with psychology has been equally noteworthy. As a research scholar, her focus has been on exploring the intricate tapestry of the human psyche, aiming to unlock the potential for psychological well-being and societal harmony. Her scholarly work is complemented by her active involvement in social work, where she employs her academic insights to make tangible differences in the lives of the underprivileged. Her endeavours in social work are characterized by an innovative approach that combines traditional wisdom with contemporary psychological practices to address the multifaceted challenges faced by these communities.

Her artistic talents, another facet of her diverse capabilities, are not merely a personal passion but also serve as a medium through which she communicates and connects with others. Her art, rich in symbolism and emotional depth, reflects her philosophical inquiries and social concerns, offering viewers a glimpse into the breadth of her intellect and the depth of her compassion.

In addition to her contributions to the arts and social sciences, Dr. Minakshi has embraced the healing arts of Pranic Healing, mastering the techniques developed by Master Choa Kok Sui. This practice, which focuses on the manipulation of Prana or life energy to heal the body and aura, has been both a personal journey of discovery and a means through which she extends her healing touch to others. Her proficiency in Pranic Healing is complemented by her advocacy and teaching of various forms of meditation aimed at rejuvenation, personal betterment, and the cultivation of harmony within individuals and communities alike.

Dr. Minakshi's life is a narrative of relentless pursuit, not just of personal achievement but of the upliftment and empowerment of society at large. Her diverse interests and talents—spanning the arts, literature, psychology, and the healing practices—converge on a singular path of service. She embodies the spirit of the luminaries who inspired her, channelling their legacy through her actions and teachings. Through her books, art, and social initiatives, she continues to inspire a new generation to embark on their own journeys of self-discovery, resilience, and altruism.

Her commitment to social betterment, particularly her focus on uplifting underprivileged children, reflects a deep understanding of the transformative potential of education and personal development. By integrating her knowledge of psychology, her artistic sensibilities, and her healing practices, Dr. Bansal has developed a holistic approach to social work that addresses both the immediate needs and the long-term well-being of the communities she serves.

As an author, Dr. Minakshi's writings offer a blend of inspirational insights, practical wisdom, and reflective contemplations drawn from her extensive reading and life experiences. Her books serve as a guide for those seeking to navigate the complexities of life with grace, resilience, and purpose. Through her narratives, she extends an invitation to her readers to explore the depths of their own potential and to contribute meaningfully to the collective well-being of society.

In Dr. Minakshi Bansal, we find a remarkable synthesis of the artist, the scholar, the healer, and the social activist. Her life's work stands as a beacon of hope and a source of inspiration for individuals seeking to make a difference in the world. Her story is a compelling reminder of the power of individual action, rooted in compassion and driven by a profound commitment to the betterment of humanity. Dr. Minakshi's legacy is not just in the tangible outcomes of her efforts but in the enduring spirit of inquiry, empathy, and service that she embodies.

❧❧❧

Preface

In a world that often emphasizes individual achievement and competition, the power of connection and collaboration remains an untapped wellspring of potential, especially for women. It is with this conviction that I embark on this exploration of networking and strategic alliances, seeking to illuminate a path towards greater empowerment and shared success for women across all spheres of life.

This book is not a mere collection of networking tips or a guide to climbing the corporate ladder. It is an invitation to reimagine the way we connect, collaborate, and build relationships. It is a call to embrace our authentic selves, to step into our power, and to leverage the collective strength of women's networks to create lasting change.

As a woman who has navigated the complexities of the professional world, I have witnessed firsthand the transformative power of meaningful connections. I have seen how a single conversation can spark a new idea, how a chance encounter can lead to a dream job, and how a supportive network can provide the courage to pursue our wildest aspirations. I have also seen the unique challenges that women face in building and maintaining professional relationships, from gender bias and microaggressions to the lack of representation in leadership positions.

It is my hope that this book will serve as a guide and inspiration for women who are seeking to build a strong support system, expand their network, and achieve their goals. Whether you are a seasoned professional or just starting out in your career, the principles and practices outlined in this book can help you to cultivate authentic relationships, navigate the complexities of the professional world, and unlock your full potential.

Throughout this book, we will explore the various facets of networking and strategic alliances, from the art of conversation and the power of mentorship to the importance of celebrating success and paying it forward. We will delve into the challenges and opportunities that women face in building and maintaining professional relationships, and we will offer practical strategies for overcoming these obstacles.

We will also explore the transformative power of collective action, the importance of building community and connection, and the role of technology in expanding our networks and amplifying our voices. We will celebrate the successes of women who have built thriving careers through strategic alliances, and we will draw inspiration from their stories.

Ultimately, this book is about more than just networking. It is about building a movement of empowered women who support each other, lift each other up, and create a more equitable and just world. It is about recognizing that our individual success is inextricably linked to the success of others, and that by working together, we can achieve far more than we ever could alone.

I invite you to join me on this journey of discovery, as we explore the power of networking and strategic alliances to transform our lives, our careers, and the world around us. Together, we can build a brighter future for ourselves and for generations to come.

Dr. Minakshi Bansal
Social Activist
Ahmedabad, Gujarat, Bharat

ONE

Beyond the Business Card: Redefining Networking for Women

The term "networking" often conjures images of awkward cocktail hours, forced conversations, and an endless exchange of business cards. However, for women, networking can be so much more than a transactional endeavor. It is an opportunity to build genuine connections, cultivate meaningful relationships, and create a supportive community that empowers personal and professional growth.

Traditionally, networking has been viewed as a linear process, focused on accumulating contacts and leveraging those connections for career advancement. However, this approach often neglects the importance of building authentic relationships based on trust, mutual respect, and shared values. Women, in particular, thrive in environments that foster collaboration, mentorship, and a sense of belonging. By redefining networking as a relational practice, women can unlock a world of opportunities that go beyond the mere exchange of business cards.

One of the key aspects of redefining networking for women is shifting the focus from quantity to quality. It's not about how many contacts you have, but rather the depth and strength of those connections. Building a few meaningful relationships can be far more valuable than collecting a stack of business cards from people you barely know. Investing time and energy in nurturing these relationships can lead to lasting friendships, mentorship opportunities, and valuable career advice.

Another crucial element of redefining networking is embracing authenticity. Women often feel pressure to conform to certain expectations or behaviors in professional settings. However, building genuine connections requires showing up as your true self. Sharing your passions, vulnerabilities, and unique perspectives can attract like-minded individuals who appreciate your authenticity. By being true to yourself, you can create a network of people who genuinely support and uplift you.

Building a strong network also involves stepping outside your comfort zone. This could mean attending industry events, joining professional organizations, or volunteering for causes you care about. By expanding your circle of contacts, you increase your chances of meeting people who can offer new perspectives, insights, and opportunities. It's important to remember that networking isn't just about what you can gain, but also what you can contribute. By offering your expertise, knowledge, and support to others, you can build a reputation as a valuable member of your community.

In the digital age, online platforms have revolutionized the way we connect with others. Social media platforms, professional networking sites, and online communities offer endless opportunities to expand your network and build relationships with people from all over the world. However, it's important to remember that online interactions should complement, not replace, in-person connections. Building trust and rapport often requires face-to-face interactions, where you can fully engage with someone's energy, body language, and nonverbal cues.

Mentorship plays a crucial role in redefining networking for women. Having a mentor can provide invaluable guidance, support, and encouragement as you navigate your career path. A mentor can offer insights, share their experiences, and help you identify and overcome challenges. Conversely, becoming a mentor allows you to give back to your community and empower the next generation of women leaders. By fostering a culture of mentorship, we can create a powerful network of women who lift each other up and achieve collective success.

Redefining networking for women also involves challenging traditional power structures and creating more inclusive spaces. Historically, networking has been dominated by men, often excluding women from important conversations and opportunities. By actively seeking out and supporting women-led initiatives, we can create a more equitable playing field and ensure that women's voices are heard. This could involve attending women-focused conferences, joining women's business groups, or participating in mentorship programs designed to empower women.

Ultimately, redefining networking for women is about creating a supportive community that fosters personal and professional growth. It's about building genuine relationships based on trust, mutual respect, and shared values. By embracing authenticity, stepping outside our comfort zones, and supporting each other, we can create a powerful network that empowers women to achieve their full potential. Remember, networking is not just about exchanging business cards, it's about building bridges, creating opportunities, and making a lasting impact on the world.

❦❦❦

Networking is not a numbers game; it's a symphony of genuine connections. Seek depth, not breadth, and cultivate relationships that resonate with your values. Remember, a few strong connections can outshine a multitude of superficial ones.

TWO

THE POWER OF CONNECTION: UNLOCKING THE POTENTIAL OF WOMEN'S NETWORKS

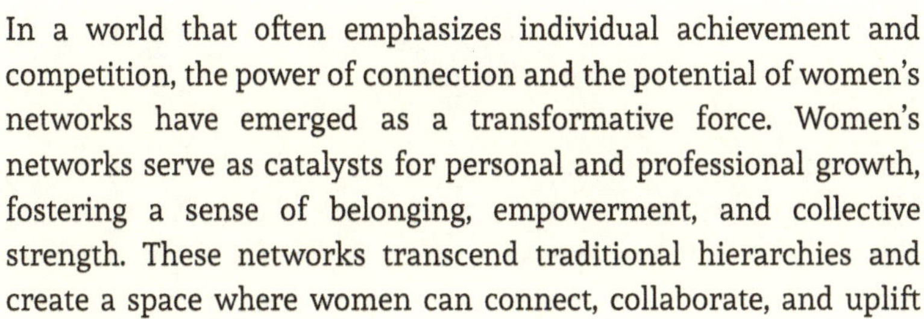

In a world that often emphasizes individual achievement and competition, the power of connection and the potential of women's networks have emerged as a transformative force. Women's networks serve as catalysts for personal and professional growth, fostering a sense of belonging, empowerment, and collective strength. These networks transcend traditional hierarchies and create a space where women can connect, collaborate, and uplift one another.

Women's networks are not merely social gatherings or casual acquaintanceships. They are intentional communities built on shared experiences, mutual support, and a common desire to break down barriers. Within these networks, women find a safe haven to share their challenges, celebrate their successes, and learn from one another. The power of these connections lies in the ability to create a sense of belonging, a place where women feel seen, heard, and valued for who they are.

One of the most significant ways women's networks unlock potential is through the exchange of knowledge and expertise. In these spaces, women can share their insights, experiences, and lessons learned, creating a collective wisdom that benefits everyone involved. This knowledge-sharing not only enhances individual growth but also fuels innovation and creativity within the network. Whether it's through formal mentorship programs, informal conversations, or online platforms, women's networks provide a wealth of information and resources that empower women to reach new heights.

Another crucial aspect of women's networks is the power of advocacy and support. Within these networks, women find allies who champion their goals, amplify their voices, and provide a much-needed support system. This support can be instrumental in navigating challenges, overcoming obstacles, and achieving personal and professional aspirations. Women's networks often serve as a sounding board for ideas, a source of encouragement, and a safe space to seek advice and guidance.

Furthermore, women's networks play a vital role in promoting leadership development and career advancement. By connecting women with mentors, sponsors, and role models, these networks create pathways to success that may not have been accessible otherwise. Women can learn from the experiences of those who have paved the way before them, gain valuable insights into leadership strategies, and develop the skills necessary to thrive in their chosen fields. Through workshops, training programs, and networking events, women's networks equip women with the tools and confidence to take on leadership roles and make a lasting impact.

The impact of women's networks extends beyond individual growth and empowerment. These networks have the power to drive social change and create a more equitable world. By amplifying women's voices, advocating for policies that support women's rights, and challenging gender stereotypes, women's networks contribute to a broader movement for gender equality. These networks also serve as incubators for social entrepreneurship, providing a platform for women to launch businesses, nonprofits, and initiatives that address critical social issues.

In the digital age, the power of women's networks has been amplified through online platforms and social media. These virtual spaces have created new avenues for connection, collaboration, and community-building. Women from all over the world can now connect with like-minded individuals, share their stories, and access resources that were previously unavailable. Online networks have also played a crucial role in mobilizing women around social causes, advocating for policy change, and creating a global movement for gender equality.

While the benefits of women's networks are undeniable, it's important to acknowledge that building and sustaining these networks requires intentional effort. It takes time, commitment, and a willingness to invest in relationships. Women must actively seek out opportunities to connect with other women, participate in network events, and contribute their unique talents and perspectives. By fostering a culture of inclusivity, generosity, and mutual support, women can create networks that thrive and empower generations to come.

In conclusion, the power of connection and the potential of

women's networks are a force to be reckoned with. These networks create a sense of belonging, empowerment, and collective strength that propels women towards personal and professional success. Through the exchange of knowledge, advocacy, leadership development, and social impact, women's networks are transforming lives and shaping a more equitable future. By embracing the power of connection, women can unlock their full potential and create a world where all women thrive.

ppp

*In the tapestry of women's networks, each thread
represents a unique story, a wealth of knowledge,
and a source of unwavering support. By weaving
our threads together, we create a vibrant and
resilient community that empowers us all to thrive.*

THREE

Building Bridges: Creating Strategic Alliances for Mutual Success

In the ever-evolving landscape of business and personal growth, the concept of strategic alliances has emerged as a powerful tool for achieving mutual success. These alliances, formed through intentional collaborations between individuals or organizations, transcend traditional boundaries and unlock a wealth of opportunities. By building bridges and forging connections, women can leverage their collective strengths, resources, and expertise to achieve goals that would be otherwise unattainable alone.

Strategic alliances are not simply transactional partnerships; they are dynamic relationships built on trust, shared values, and a common vision. They require a willingness to collaborate, to listen, and to compromise. When women come together to form strategic alliances, they create a synergistic force that can propel them towards greater heights. These alliances can take many forms, from formal partnerships between businesses to informal collaborations between individuals. Regardless of the structure, the underlying principle remains the same: by working together, we can achieve more than we ever could alone.

One of the key benefits of strategic alliances is the ability to leverage complementary strengths. Each individual or organization brings unique skills, knowledge, and resources to the table. By combining these assets, alliances can create a powerful synergy that amplifies their impact. For example, a woman with expertise in marketing may partner with a woman who excels in finance, creating a well-rounded team that can tackle a wider range of challenges. By recognizing and valuing each other's strengths, women can build alliances that maximize their collective potential.

Strategic alliances also provide access to new markets and opportunities. By partnering with individuals or organizations that have established networks and connections, women can expand their reach and tap into previously untapped resources. This can be particularly beneficial for women entrepreneurs and small business owners who may lack the resources or connections to break into new markets on their own. Through strategic alliances, they can gain access to valuable distribution channels, marketing expertise, and financial support, accelerating their growth and increasing their chances of success.

In addition to tangible benefits, strategic alliances also offer intangible rewards. By collaborating with others, women can expand their knowledge base, gain new perspectives, and learn from the experiences of others. This cross-pollination of ideas can spark innovation, creativity, and personal growth. Furthermore, strategic alliances can provide a sense of community and belonging, creating a supportive network of individuals who share similar goals and challenges. This sense of camaraderie can be invaluable, especially for women who may face unique obstacles in their personal or professional lives.

Building successful strategic alliances requires careful planning and execution. It's important to identify potential partners who share your values, goals, and vision. This can involve conducting thorough research, attending networking events, and building relationships with key stakeholders. Once potential partners have been identified, it's crucial to establish clear expectations, define roles and responsibilities, and create a communication plan that ensures everyone is on the same page.

Transparency and open communication are essential for the success of any strategic alliance. By fostering a culture of trust and mutual respect, women can create partnerships that are built to last. Regular check-ins, progress reports, and open dialogue can help identify and address any issues that may arise. It's also important to celebrate successes and recognize the contributions of each partner. By acknowledging and appreciating each other's efforts, women can create a positive and rewarding alliance experience.

The power of strategic alliances extends beyond the individual level. When women come together to form alliances, they create a collective force that can drive social change and empower communities. By pooling their resources and expertise, women can tackle complex challenges, advocate for policy change, and create a more equitable world. For example, women-led organizations have formed alliances to address issues such as gender-based violence, climate change, and economic inequality. These alliances have amplified women's voices, mobilized resources, and created a powerful platform for social change.

In conclusion, building bridges through strategic alliances is a powerful strategy for achieving mutual success. By leveraging complementary strengths, accessing new markets, and fostering a sense of community, women can unlock a wealth of opportunities that would be otherwise unattainable alone. These alliances require careful planning, open communication, and a commitment to shared values. When women come together to form strategic alliances, they create a force for good that can transform lives, empower communities, and create a more equitable world.

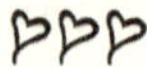

Strategic alliances are not just business arrangements; they are transformative partnerships built on trust, shared vision, and mutual benefit. When women unite their strengths, they unleash a collective power that can reshape industries and drive meaningful change.

FOUR

Navigating the Landscape: Women in Networking and Leadership

The landscape of networking and leadership presents a unique set of challenges and opportunities for women. While progress has been made in recent decades, women continue to face systemic barriers and biases that can hinder their advancement in both professional and personal spheres. However, by understanding the landscape, developing effective strategies, and leveraging their unique strengths, women can navigate this terrain with confidence and achieve remarkable success.

One of the key challenges women face in networking and leadership is the persistence of gender stereotypes and unconscious biases. These biases can manifest in subtle ways, such as being overlooked for promotions, receiving less credit for their contributions, or being underestimated in their abilities. To navigate this landscape, women must be aware of these biases and develop strategies to counteract them. This can involve advocating for themselves, building strong relationships with mentors and sponsors, and actively seeking out opportunities to showcase their skills and expertise.

Another challenge women face is the lack of representation in leadership positions. Despite making up a significant portion of the workforce, women remain underrepresented in senior management roles. This lack of representation can create a sense of isolation and make it difficult for women to envision themselves as leaders. To overcome this challenge, women can seek out role models and mentors who can provide guidance and support. They can also participate in leadership development programs and actively seek out opportunities to take on leadership roles within their organizations.

Networking plays a crucial role in navigating the landscape for women in leadership. By building strong relationships with other women, as well as men who are allies, women can create a supportive network that can provide valuable resources, advice, and opportunities. Networking can also help women to build their visibility and reputation within their industry or field. By attending industry events, participating in professional organizations, and engaging in online communities, women can expand their circle of influence and create new opportunities for collaboration and advancement.

Leadership styles also play a significant role in how women navigate the landscape. While there is no one-size-fits-all approach, research suggests that women often adopt a more collaborative and transformational leadership style. This style emphasizes building relationships, empowering others, and creating a shared vision for the future. By embracing their unique strengths and leadership styles, women can create a more inclusive and supportive work environment that benefits everyone.

Mentorship and sponsorship are also critical components of navigating the landscape for women in leadership. Mentors can provide guidance, advice, and support, while sponsors can advocate for women and help them to advance their careers. By seeking out mentors and sponsors, women can gain valuable insights, access to new opportunities, and a greater sense of confidence in their abilities.

Technology has also played a significant role in shaping the landscape for women in networking and leadership. Online platforms and social media have created new avenues for connection, collaboration, and community-building. By leveraging these tools, women can expand their networks, access resources, and amplify their voices. However, it's important to be mindful of the potential pitfalls of online interactions, such as cyberbullying and harassment. By using technology wisely and setting boundaries, women can harness the power of online platforms to advance their careers and achieve their goals.

In conclusion, navigating the landscape for women in networking and leadership requires a multifaceted approach. By understanding the challenges, developing effective strategies, and leveraging their unique strengths, women can overcome barriers and achieve remarkable success. Building strong networks, seeking out mentors and sponsors, embracing their leadership styles, and utilizing technology wisely are all key components of this journey. By working together and supporting each other, women can create a more inclusive and equitable landscape for future generations of leaders.

Navigating the landscape of leadership requires more than just skills and ambition. It demands resilience, authenticity, and a commitment to lifting others as you climb. Remember, true leadership is not about power over others, but about empowering others to reach their full potential.

FIVE

AUTHENTICITY IN ACTION: CULTIVATING MEANINGFUL PROFESSIONAL RELATIONSHIPS

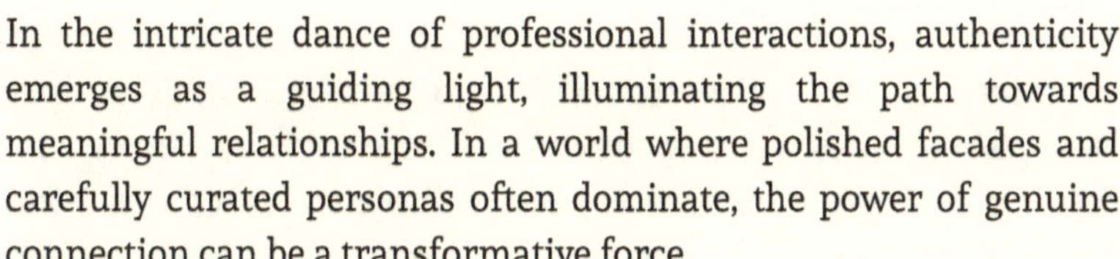

In the intricate dance of professional interactions, authenticity emerges as a guiding light, illuminating the path towards meaningful relationships. In a world where polished facades and carefully curated personas often dominate, the power of genuine connection can be a transformative force.

By embracing authenticity in our professional lives, we unlock a deeper level of engagement, trust, and collaboration that fuels both personal and collective success.

Authenticity, at its core, is about aligning our actions with our values, beliefs, and true selves. It is about showing up as our genuine selves, both in our words and in our deeds. In the professional realm, this means being transparent about our intentions, communicating openly and honestly, and embracing our unique strengths and weaknesses.

While it may seem counterintuitive in a competitive environment, authenticity can be a powerful differentiator, setting us apart from the crowd and attracting like-minded individuals who appreciate our genuine approach.

Cultivating meaningful professional relationships begins with self-awareness. To be authentic, we must first understand who we are, what we stand for, and what we want to achieve. This involves introspection, reflection, and a willingness to confront our own biases and limitations. By understanding our values and motivations, we can make conscious choices that align with our true selves, both in our personal and professional lives.

Once we have a clear understanding of ourselves, we can begin to build authentic connections with others. This involves being present and engaged in our interactions, listening actively to others, and expressing our thoughts and feelings honestly and respectfully.

It also means being vulnerable, sharing our experiences and perspectives, and allowing others to see our human side. Vulnerability can be a powerful tool for building trust and connection, as it demonstrates our willingness to be open and honest with others.

Authenticity in action also means embracing our unique strengths and weaknesses. We all have different talents, skills, and experiences to offer. By recognizing and valuing our individual contributions, we can create a more diverse and inclusive workplace where everyone feels valued and respected. It's important to remember that authenticity doesn't mean being perfect; it means being honest about our imperfections and striving to learn and grow from our mistakes.

In the digital age, where much of our communication takes place online, authenticity can be particularly challenging. Social media platforms and professional networking sites often encourage us to present a carefully curated image of ourselves.

However, it's important to remember that true connection happens when we are willing to show up as our authentic selves, even in the virtual world. This can involve sharing personal stories, expressing our opinions, and engaging in meaningful conversations with others.

Building meaningful professional relationships takes time and effort. It requires consistent communication, mutual respect, and a willingness to invest in the relationship. It also means setting boundaries, being mindful of our own needs, and knowing when to walk away from relationships that are not serving us. By prioritizing quality over quantity, we can cultivate a network of authentic connections that support our personal and professional growth.

The benefits of authenticity in the workplace are numerous. Authentic leaders inspire trust, loyalty, and engagement among their team members.

They create a culture of openness and collaboration where everyone feels safe to share their ideas and contribute their unique talents. Authentic relationships also lead to increased productivity, innovation, and job satisfaction. When people feel valued and respected for who they are, they are more likely to be motivated and engaged in their work.

In conclusion, authenticity in action is the key to cultivating meaningful professional relationships. By aligning our actions with our values, embracing our unique strengths and weaknesses, and building genuine connections with others, we can create a more fulfilling and successful professional life. Authenticity is not just a buzzword; it is a way of being that can transform our relationships, our careers, and our lives.

ϷϷϷ

Authenticity is the key that unlocks the door to meaningful connections. Embrace your unique voice, share your story, and let your true self shine through. In a world that often values conformity, dare to be different, and attract a network that celebrates your individuality.

SIX

THE ART OF CONVERSATION: MASTERING THE SKILLS OF EFFECTIVE NETWORKING

Networking, at its heart, is about building relationships. And the foundation of any relationship is communication. The art of conversation is a powerful tool in the networking arsenal, enabling individuals to forge genuine connections, establish trust, and unlock a world of opportunities.

By mastering the skills of effective networking conversations, we can create lasting impressions, expand our professional circles, and achieve our goals.

Effective networking conversations go beyond mere small talk or exchanging pleasantries. They are intentional interactions that aim to create meaningful connections and leave a lasting impact. A successful networking conversation involves active listening, thoughtful questions, and the ability to articulate our own ideas and experiences in a compelling way.

It's about finding common ground, building rapport, and leaving a positive impression that opens doors to future opportunities.

One of the most critical skills in networking conversations is active listening. It's not just about hearing the words that someone is saying; it's about truly understanding their message, their perspective, and their needs.

Active listening involves paying attention to both verbal and nonverbal cues, asking clarifying questions, and reflecting back what we've heard to ensure understanding. By demonstrating genuine interest in others and their stories, we can build rapport and create a deeper level of connection.

Asking thoughtful questions is another key component of effective networking conversations. Open-ended questions that encourage others to share their experiences, insights, and aspirations can lead to meaningful discussions and uncover hidden opportunities.

By asking questions that go beyond the surface level, we can gain a deeper understanding of others and their motivations, which can be invaluable in building strong relationships.

In addition to listening and asking questions, it's important to be able to articulate our own ideas and experiences in a clear and compelling way. This involves crafting a concise and engaging elevator pitch that highlights our unique value proposition. It also means being able to tell our story in a way that resonates with others and leaves a lasting impression. By sharing our passions, challenges, and successes, we can create a sense of authenticity and build trust with others.

Networking conversations are not just about what we say; they're also about how we say it. Nonverbal communication, such as body language, facial expressions, and tone of voice, plays a crucial role in conveying our message and building rapport.

Maintaining eye contact, smiling, and using open body language can signal warmth, approachability, and confidence. Conversely, crossed arms, a furrowed brow, or a monotone voice can convey disinterest or negativity. By being mindful of our nonverbal cues, we can create a positive and engaging communication experience.

Effective networking conversations also involve a degree of reciprocity. It's not just about what we can get from others; it's also about what we can offer. By sharing our knowledge, expertise, and resources, we can create a sense of mutual benefit and build stronger relationships. This can involve offering to connect someone with a relevant contact, providing helpful advice or feedback, or simply being a supportive listener.

By demonstrating our willingness to contribute, we can establish ourselves as valuable members of our network.

In the digital age, networking conversations often take place online. While virtual interactions lack the same level of intimacy as face-to-face encounters, they still offer valuable opportunities to connect with others and build relationships.

When engaging in online conversations, it's important to be mindful of our tone, language, and overall communication style. A well-crafted email, a thoughtful LinkedIn message, or an engaging comment on a social media post can all contribute to building a strong online presence and expanding our network.

Ultimately, the art of conversation is about creating genuine connections with others. By actively listening, asking thoughtful questions, articulating our own ideas, and demonstrating a willingness to contribute, we can build relationships that open doors to new opportunities and enrich our lives. Networking conversations are not just about exchanging information; they're about building trust, fostering collaboration, and creating a community of support.

By mastering the skills of effective networking conversations, we can unlock our full potential and achieve our goals.

The art of conversation is a powerful tool for building relationships and creating opportunities. Listen actively, ask thoughtful questions, and share your insights with generosity. Remember, every conversation is a chance to learn, grow, and make a lasting impression.

SEVEN

Mentorship Matters: Empowering Women Through Guidance and Support

In the intricate tapestry of personal and professional development, mentorship emerges as a guiding thread, weaving together experience, wisdom, and support to empower women on their journey toward success. It is a relationship that transcends mere advice-giving, fostering a deep connection between individuals where knowledge is shared, skills are honed, and confidence is nurtured. For women, mentorship can be a transformative force, providing the guidance and support needed to navigate challenges, seize opportunities, and reach their full potential.

At its core, mentorship is a reciprocal relationship built on trust, respect, and a shared desire for growth. A mentor, typically someone with more experience and expertise, offers guidance, insights, and encouragement to a mentee, who is eager to learn and develop. This relationship can take many forms, from formal programs within organizations to informal connections forged through shared interests or networks. Regardless of the structure, the essence of mentorship lies in the power of human connection and the willingness to share knowledge and experience.

For women, mentorship can be particularly impactful. Throughout history, women have faced systemic barriers and biases that have hindered their access to opportunities and advancement. Mentorship can serve as a counterbalance to these challenges, providing women with the support and guidance needed to overcome obstacles and achieve their goals. A mentor can offer a unique perspective, sharing their own experiences and lessons learned, and providing a roadmap for navigating the complexities of the professional world.

One of the most significant ways mentorship empowers women is through the transfer of knowledge and skills. A mentor can share their expertise, insights, and best practices, helping their mentee to develop new competencies and enhance existing ones. This can be particularly valuable for women who may lack access to formal training or development programs. Through mentorship, women can gain the skills and knowledge needed to succeed in their chosen field, whether it's leadership, communication, negotiation, or technical expertise.

Mentorship also plays a crucial role in building confidence and self-efficacy. A mentor can provide encouragement, affirmation, and constructive feedback, helping their mentee to recognize their strengths and overcome their weaknesses. By believing in their mentee's potential and offering unwavering support, a mentor can help to instill a sense of confidence that can propel them towards success. This is especially important for women, who may face societal pressures and internalized doubts that can undermine their self-belief.

Another key benefit of mentorship is the access it provides to networks and opportunities. A mentor can introduce their mentee to key contacts, open doors to new experiences, and provide valuable insights into the unwritten rules of their industry or field. This can be particularly beneficial for women who may face challenges in building their professional networks due to gender bias or lack of access to informal channels of information. Through mentorship, women can gain access to the resources and connections needed to advance their careers and achieve their goals.

Mentorship can also provide a safe space for women to discuss challenges and seek guidance on sensitive issues. A mentor can offer a confidential and supportive environment where women can share their experiences, concerns, and aspirations without fear of judgment or reprisal. This can be particularly important for women who may face unique challenges related to work-life balance, discrimination, or harassment. By providing a safe space for open and honest dialogue, mentorship can help women to process their experiences, develop coping mechanisms, and find solutions to their challenges.

While the benefits of mentorship are undeniable, it's important to recognize that not all mentorship relationships are created equal. A successful mentorship relationship requires a good fit between mentor and mentee, based on shared values, interests, and goals. It also requires a commitment from both parties to invest time and effort in the relationship. Finding the right mentor can be a challenge, but it's worth the effort. By seeking out mentors who are genuinely invested in their mentee's success, women can create powerful partnerships that can transform their lives.

In conclusion, mentorship matters. It is a powerful tool for empowering women through guidance, support, and access to opportunities. By sharing their knowledge, experience, and networks, mentors can help women to overcome challenges, build confidence, and achieve their full potential. Mentorship is not just about career advancement; it's about personal growth, empowerment, and creating a more equitable world. By investing in mentorship relationships, we can create a ripple effect of positive change that will benefit generations to come.

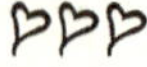

Mentorship is a gift that keeps on giving. Whether you are a mentor or a mentee, the exchange of knowledge, experience, and support can be transformative. Embrace the opportunity to learn from those who have gone before you, and pay it forward by guiding and empowering the next generation.

EIGHT

BREAKING BARRIERS: OVERCOMING CHALLENGES IN BUILDING ALLIANCES

The path to building strong ad impactful alliances is rarely a smooth one. It is often paved with challenges and obstacles that can hinder progress and discourage collaboration. However, by recognizing these barriers and developing effective strategies to overcome them, women can forge powerful alliances that lead to mutual success and create lasting change.

One of the most significant barriers to building alliances is the fear of vulnerability. Opening up to others, sharing our ideas, and exposing our vulnerabilities can be daunting, especially in a competitive environment. We may fear judgment, rejection, or even exploitation. However, vulnerability is a necessary component of building trust, which is the foundation of any successful alliance.

By being willing to share our authentic selves, we create an environment where others feel safe to do the same, fostering deeper connections and stronger collaborations.

Another common challenge is the lack of trust. Trust is not something that can be built overnight; it requires time, consistency, and a demonstrated commitment to mutual benefit. In the early stages of alliance building, it's important to establish clear expectations, define roles and responsibilities, and create a communication plan that ensures everyone is on the same page. Transparency and open communication are essential for building trust and ensuring that all parties feel heard and valued.

Differences in communication styles and personalities can also pose a challenge to alliance building. We all have unique ways of communicating and interacting with others. Misunderstandings and conflicts can arise when these differences are not acknowledged and addressed. To overcome this challenge, it's important to practice active listening, seek to understand different perspectives, and find common ground. By embracing diversity and valuing different communication styles, we can create alliances that are more resilient and adaptable.

Competition can also be a barrier to alliance building. In a world that often emphasizes individual achievement, it can be difficult to shift our mindset towards collaboration. We may fear that by partnering with others, we will lose our competitive edge or be overshadowed by our partners. However, competition and collaboration are not mutually exclusive. By recognizing that we can achieve more together than we ever could alone, we can embrace collaboration as a strategy for mutual success.

Limited resources can also present a challenge to alliance building. Whether it's time, money, or expertise, resources are often finite. When building alliances, it's important to be mindful of these limitations and prioritize activities that will yield the greatest impact. By pooling resources, sharing expertise, and leveraging each other's strengths, we can maximize our collective impact and achieve our goals more efficiently.

In addition to these internal barriers, there may also be external factors that can hinder alliance building. These can include political or regulatory constraints, cultural differences, or even simple logistical challenges. To overcome these external barriers, it's important to be adaptable, creative, and persistent. By seeking out common ground, building bridges across differences, and finding innovative solutions to challenges, we can overcome external obstacles and forge lasting alliances.

Building successful alliances requires a combination of skills, strategies, and mindset shifts. It's about recognizing our own vulnerabilities, building trust, embracing diversity, and finding common ground. It's about prioritizing collaboration over competition, leveraging our collective strengths, and finding creative solutions to challenges. By breaking down barriers and overcoming obstacles, we can create powerful alliances that empower women, drive social change, and create a more equitable world.

The journey of alliance building is not always easy, but it is undoubtedly rewarding. By embracing the challenges and opportunities that come with collaboration, we can create a brighter future for ourselves and for generations to come.

ÞÞÞ

Building alliances is not always easy, but the rewards are worth the effort. Embrace vulnerability, build trust, and seek common ground. Remember, collaboration is not about compromising your values, but about finding creative solutions that benefit everyone involved.

NINE

LEVERAGING TECHNOLOGY: EXPANDING YOUR NETWORK IN THE DIGITAL AGE

In the digital age, technology has revolutionized the way we connect, communicate, and build relationships. The rise of social media, professional networking platforms, and online communities has opened up a world of possibilities for expanding our networks and forging meaningful connections with people from all corners of the globe. For women, who have historically faced barriers to traditional networking opportunities, leveraging technology can be a game-changer, providing access to a diverse range of connections and resources that can propel their personal and professional growth.

One of the most powerful tools for expanding your network in the digital age is social media. Platforms like LinkedIn, Twitter, and

Facebook offer a wealth of opportunities to connect with like-minded individuals, industry leaders, and potential mentors. By actively engaging in online conversations, sharing valuable content, and building a strong personal brand, women can establish themselves as thought leaders and attract a following of individuals who share their interests and values. Social media also provides a platform for joining groups and communities focused on specific industries, interests, or causes, allowing women to connect with others who share their passions and goals.

Professional networking platforms like LinkedIn have become indispensable tools for building and maintaining professional relationships. These platforms allow users to create detailed profiles showcasing their skills, experience, and accomplishments. They also provide opportunities to connect with colleagues, alumni, and industry leaders, join groups and discussions, and access job postings and career resources. By actively using LinkedIn, women can expand their network, build their personal brand, and stay informed about industry trends and opportunities.

Online communities and forums offer another avenue for expanding your network and connecting with people who share your interests and goals. These platforms provide a space for discussions, knowledge sharing, and collaboration. By participating in these communities, women can gain valuable insights, build relationships with potential mentors or collaborators, and stay abreast of the latest developments in their field. Online communities can also be a source of support and encouragement, providing a safe space for women to share their experiences, challenges, and successes.

In addition to social media and networking platforms, technology has also enabled the rise of virtual events and conferences. These events offer a convenient and accessible way to connect with people from all over the world, learn from experts, and build relationships with potential clients, partners, or employers. By attending virtual events, women can expand their knowledge, gain new perspectives, and make valuable connections without the constraints of travel or time.

While technology offers a wealth of opportunities for expanding your network, it's important to be intentional and strategic in your approach. Simply having a presence on social media or joining a few online communities is not enough. To truly leverage technology for networking, you need to actively engage with others, share valuable content, and build genuine relationships. This involves taking the time to get to know people, offering support and encouragement, and seeking out opportunities for collaboration.

It's also important to be mindful of your online presence and personal brand. In the digital age, your online reputation can have a significant impact on your career prospects. By curating a professional online profile, sharing thoughtful content, and engaging in positive interactions, you can build a strong personal brand that attracts opportunities and opens doors.

In conclusion, leveraging technology to expand your network in the digital age is a powerful strategy for personal and professional growth. By utilizing social media, professional networking platforms, online communities, and virtual events, women can overcome traditional barriers to networking and build a diverse and supportive network of connections. However, it's important to be intentional and strategic in your approach, actively engaging with others, building genuine relationships, and curating a strong personal brand. By harnessing the power of technology, women can unlock a world of opportunities and achieve their full potential.

ϼϼϼ

Technology is a powerful tool for expanding your network and connecting with like-minded individuals. Leverage social media, online communities, and virtual events to build a global network of support and inspiration. But remember, true connection often requires face-to-face interactions, so don't neglect the power of personal touch.

TEN

FINDING YOUR TRIBE: BUILDING COMMUNITY AND CONNECTION

In the vast landscape of human interaction, the concept of finding one's "tribe" resonates deeply. It speaks to the innate human desire for belonging, for connection with others who share our values, interests, and passions. For women, the journey of finding their tribe can be a transformative experience, leading to personal growth, empowerment, and a sense of purpose. By building community and fostering connections with like-minded individuals, women can create a supportive network that nurtures their dreams, amplifies their voices, and propels them towards success.

Finding your tribe is not about conforming to a particular mold or fitting into a predefined category. It's about discovering and embracing your authentic self, and then seeking out others who resonate with your values and aspirations. It's about creating a space where you feel seen, heard, and understood, where you can share your joys, challenges, and vulnerabilities without fear of judgment.

Building community and connection starts with self-reflection. Take the time to explore your passions, interests, and values. What are you truly passionate about? What activities bring you joy and fulfillment? What causes do you care deeply about? By understanding yourself and what you value, you can begin to identify communities and individuals who align with your vision of the world.

Once you have a clearer sense of who you are and what you seek, start exploring different avenues for connection. This could involve joining professional organizations, attending industry events, volunteering for causes you care about, or participating in online communities and forums. The key is to put yourself out there, engage with others, and be open to new experiences.

Building community is not just about attending events or joining groups; it's about actively participating and contributing. Share your knowledge, insights, and experiences with others. Offer support and encouragement to those who are just starting out. Celebrate the successes of others and learn from their challenges. By actively engaging with your community, you can build stronger connections and create a sense of belonging.

Technology has revolutionized the way we connect with others, opening up a world of possibilities for building community and connection. Online platforms, social media groups, and virtual events provide accessible and convenient ways to connect with like-minded individuals from all over the world. These virtual spaces can be particularly valuable for women who may face geographical or social barriers to traditional networking opportunities.

However, it's important to remember that online interactions should complement, not replace, in-person connections. While technology can facilitate initial connections, building deeper relationships often requires face-to-face interactions. This could involve attending local meetups, organizing coffee chats, or simply reaching out to someone you admire for a conversation. By investing time and effort in building personal connections, you can create a more meaningful and lasting sense of community.

Mentorship can also play a crucial role in finding your tribe. A mentor can offer guidance, support, and access to networks and opportunities that can help you to connect with the right people and build your community. By seeking out mentors who share your values and aspirations, you can gain valuable insights and accelerate your personal and professional growth.

Building community is not always easy. It takes time, effort, and a willingness to be vulnerable. There will be times when you feel discouraged or disconnected. But by persevering and staying true to yourself, you will eventually find your tribe – a group of individuals who inspire, support, and challenge you to become the best version of yourself.

In conclusion, finding your tribe is a journey of self-discovery, connection, and growth. It's about embracing your authentic self, seeking out like-minded individuals, and building a community that supports your dreams and aspirations. By actively participating, contributing, and building genuine relationships, you can create a network of support that will empower you to achieve your full potential. Remember, you are not alone. There are others out there who share your passions, values, and dreams. Find your tribe, build your community, and together, you can create a world that is more inclusive, supportive, and empowering for all.

ÞÞÞ

Finding your tribe is a journey of self-discovery and connection. Seek out communities that share your values, interests, and passions. Contribute your unique talents and perspectives, and embrace the diversity of thought and experience. Remember, belonging is not about fitting in; it's about finding your place in a community that celebrates your individuality.

ELEVEN

Amplifying Your Voice: Sharing Your Expertise and Insights

In a world overflowing with information, the ability to share your expertise and insights effectively can be a game-changer. It can open doors to new opportunities, establish you as a thought leader, and empower others with your knowledge. For women, who have historically been underrepresented in many fields, amplifying their voices is particularly crucial for driving change, challenging stereotypes, and creating a more equitable world.

Sharing your expertise and insights is not just about self-promotion; it's about making a meaningful contribution to your community and beyond. It's about empowering others with your knowledge, inspiring them to action, and fostering a culture of learning and growth.

Whether you're a seasoned professional or just starting out in your career, your unique perspective and insights have value. By sharing them, you can make a difference in the lives of others and contribute to a more informed and engaged society.

One of the most effective ways to amplify your voice is through public speaking. Whether it's giving a presentation at a conference, delivering a keynote address, or simply speaking up in a meeting, public speaking allows you to share your expertise with a wider audience. It can be a powerful platform for establishing your credibility, building your brand, and influencing others.

However, public speaking can also be intimidating, especially for women who may face additional challenges such as imposter syndrome or gender bias. By preparing thoroughly, practicing your delivery, and focusing on connecting with your audience, you can overcome these challenges and deliver a compelling and impactful message.

Writing is another powerful tool for sharing your expertise and insights. Whether it's through blog posts, articles, white papers, or even social media posts, writing allows you to express your ideas in a clear and concise way. It can also be a way to reach a wider audience and establish yourself as a thought leader in your field. By consistently creating high-quality content that resonates with your target audience, you can build a loyal following and expand your influence.

Mentoring is another way to amplify your voice and empower others with your knowledge. By sharing your experiences, insights, and advice with less experienced individuals, you can help them to develop their skills, navigate their careers, and achieve their goals. Mentoring can also be a rewarding experience for the mentor, providing an opportunity to give back to the community and make a lasting impact on the next generation of leaders.

In the digital age, social media platforms have become powerful tools for amplifying your voice and reaching a global audience. By sharing your expertise and insights on platforms like LinkedIn, Twitter, and Facebook, you can connect with like-minded individuals, spark conversations, and build a community of followers who are interested in what you have to say.

Social media also provides a platform for engaging with influencers, thought leaders, and potential collaborators, opening doors to new opportunities and partnerships.

Networking events, both in-person and virtual, can also be valuable opportunities for sharing your expertise and insights. By attending conferences, workshops, and meetups, you can connect with other professionals in your field, exchange ideas, and learn from each other. Networking events can also be a platform for showcasing your skills, building your brand, and establishing yourself as a thought leader.

However, amplifying your voice is not just about speaking or writing; it's also about listening. By actively listening to others, seeking out diverse perspectives, and engaging in meaningful conversations, you can deepen your understanding of the issues that matter most to you and your community.

Listening also allows you to build relationships with others, learn from their experiences, and identify opportunities for collaboration.

Amplifying your voice requires courage, vulnerability, and a willingness to put yourself out there. It's not always easy to share your ideas and opinions, especially when faced with potential criticism or rejection. However, by embracing vulnerability and stepping outside your comfort zone, you can unleash your full potential and make a lasting impact on the world.

In conclusion, amplifying your voice is a powerful way to share your expertise, empower others, and drive change. Whether it's through public speaking, writing, mentoring, social media, or networking events, there are countless ways to make your voice heard.

By embracing authenticity, seeking out diverse perspectives, and building relationships with others, you can create a ripple effect of positive change that extends far beyond yourself. Remember, your voice matters. Share it with the world and make a difference.

ppp

Your voice matters. Share your expertise, insights, and experiences with the world. Speak up in meetings, write articles, give presentations, and mentor others. Remember, your knowledge has the power to empower others and create positive change.

TWELVE

COLLABORATION OVER COMPETITION: EMBRACING THE POWER OF SHARED SUCCESS

In a world that often glorifies individual achievement and competition, the concept of collaboration emerges as a refreshing and powerful alternative. Collaboration, the act of working together to achieve a common goal, has the potential to unlock a wealth of benefits for individuals, organizations, and society as a whole. By embracing the power of shared success, we can break down barriers, foster innovation, and create a more equitable and sustainable world.

The traditional model of competition, where individuals or organizations strive to outperform one another, often leads to a win-lose mentality. This approach can stifle creativity, limit growth, and create a toxic environment where everyone is constantly vying for recognition and resources. In contrast, collaboration encourages a win-win mentality, where everyone involved benefits from the collective effort. By pooling resources, sharing knowledge, and leveraging each other's strengths, collaborators can achieve outcomes that would be impossible to attain alone.

One of the most significant benefits of collaboration is the increased potential for innovation. When diverse minds come together, they bring a wide range of perspectives, experiences, and ideas to the table. This diversity of thought can spark new insights, challenge assumptions, and lead to groundbreaking solutions. In a collaborative environment, individuals are encouraged to share their ideas freely, without fear of judgment or ridicule. This creates a fertile ground for creativity, where ideas can be explored, refined, and developed into tangible results.

Collaboration also fosters a sense of community and belonging. When people work together towards a common goal, they develop a shared sense of purpose and identity. This can be particularly empowering for women, who have historically been excluded from many collaborative spaces. By creating inclusive and supportive environments where women's voices are valued and their contributions are recognized, we can unlock their full potential and create a more equitable world.

In the business world, collaboration can lead to increased efficiency, productivity, and profitability. By partnering with other organizations, businesses can access new markets, share resources, and reduce costs. Collaborative projects can also lead to the development of new products and services that would not have been possible through individual efforts. For example, many successful startups have emerged from collaborations between entrepreneurs with complementary skills and expertise.

Collaboration is not just beneficial for businesses; it can also have a positive impact on society as a whole. By working together, we can tackle complex challenges such as climate change, poverty, and inequality. Collaborative initiatives can bring together diverse stakeholders, including governments, businesses, nonprofits, and community groups, to develop comprehensive solutions that address the root causes of these problems.

In the digital age, technology has made collaboration easier than ever before. Online platforms, virtual meetings, and collaborative software tools enable people from all over the world to work together seamlessly. This has opened up new possibilities for cross-cultural collaboration, allowing individuals and organizations to learn from each other and develop innovative solutions to global challenges.

However, collaboration is not without its challenges. Building trust, managing conflict, and aligning diverse interests can be difficult. It requires effective communication, a willingness to compromise, and a shared commitment to the common goal. Successful collaboration also requires strong leadership, clear roles and responsibilities, and a well-defined decision-making process.

Despite these challenges, the benefits of collaboration far outweigh the drawbacks. By embracing the power of shared success, we can break down barriers, foster innovation, and create a more equitable and sustainable world. Whether it's in the workplace, in our communities, or on a global scale, collaboration is the key to unlocking our full potential and building a brighter future for all.

ÞÞÞ

Collaboration is not a sign of weakness; it is a testament to strength. By embracing the power of shared success, we can achieve far more than we ever could alone. Remember, together, we can create a world that is more equitable, inclusive, and sustainable.

THIRTEEN

From Networking to Net-Weaving: Creating a Strong Support System

The traditional concept of networking, often associated with transactional exchanges and superficial connections, is evolving into a more profound and enriching practice known as net-weaving. This shift in perspective emphasizes the importance of building genuine relationships, fostering mutual support, and creating a strong support system that empowers individuals to thrive.

For women, net-weaving can be a transformative force, providing a sense of belonging, empowerment, and resilience in the face of challenges.

Net-weaving goes beyond simply collecting contacts or attending networking events. It involves intentionally cultivating meaningful relationships based on trust, shared values, and a genuine desire to support one another. This approach recognizes that true connections are built over time, through shared experiences, open communication, and mutual respect.

By shifting the focus from transactional networking to intentional net-weaving, women can create a powerful network of allies who will uplift, empower, and inspire them.

One of the key elements of net-weaving is the recognition that relationships are reciprocal. It's not just about what you can get from others, but also what you can give. By offering support, encouragement, and expertise to others, you create a dynamic of reciprocity that strengthens the bonds within your network. This could involve sharing your knowledge and skills, offering a listening ear, providing constructive feedback, or simply being there for someone in need.

By investing in the success and well-being of others, you create a network that is invested in your success and well-being in return.

Net-weaving also involves building relationships with individuals from diverse backgrounds and perspectives. By expanding your circle of connections beyond your immediate field or industry, you can gain access to new ideas, insights, and opportunities.

Diversity in your network can also challenge your assumptions, broaden your horizons, and help you to see the world through different lenses. By embracing diversity, you create a more vibrant and resilient network that can adapt to changing circumstances and support you through a variety of challenges.

Another important aspect of net-weaving is the willingness to be vulnerable. Building genuine relationships requires opening up to others, sharing your struggles, and asking for help when needed. Vulnerability can be scary, but it is also essential for building trust and connection.

By showing your authentic self and allowing others to see your vulnerabilities, you create a space where others feel safe to do the same. This vulnerability can lead to deeper connections and stronger bonds of support.

In the digital age, technology has opened up new avenues for net-weaving. Online communities, social media groups, and virtual events provide opportunities to connect with like-minded individuals from all over the world.

These virtual spaces can be particularly valuable for women who may face geographical or social barriers to traditional networking opportunities. By leveraging technology, women can build a global network of support that can empower them to achieve their goals and make a difference in the world.

However, it's important to remember that online interactions should complement, not replace, in-person connections. Building deep and meaningful relationships often requires face-to-face interactions, where you can fully engage with someone's energy, body language, and nonverbal cues. By balancing online and offline interactions, you can create a more holistic and effective net-weaving strategy.

Building a strong support system takes time, effort, and intentionality. It requires investing in relationships, showing up for others, and being willing to ask for help when needed. By prioritizing net-weaving over transactional networking, you can create a network of allies who will uplift, empower, and inspire you on your journey towards success.

In conclusion, net-weaving is a powerful approach to building a strong support system that can empower women to achieve their full potential. By fostering genuine connections, embracing diversity, and being willing to be vulnerable, women can create a network of allies who will support them through thick and thin.

The benefits of net-weaving are numerous, including increased access to resources, opportunities, and emotional support. By prioritizing net-weaving, women can build a community that will empower them to thrive in all aspects of their lives.

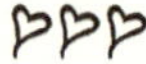

Networking is not just about collecting contacts; it's about weaving a web of support. Cultivate meaningful relationships, offer support and encouragement to others, and be open to receiving help when needed. Remember, a strong network is a source of strength, resilience, and opportunity.

FOURTEEN

CELEBRATING SUCCESS: RECOGNIZING ACHIEVEMENTS AND BUILDING MOMENTUM

In the pursuit of our goals, whether personal or professional, it is essential to not only focus on the destination but also to appreciate and celebrate the journey. Recognizing and celebrating our achievements, both big and small, is a crucial element in maintaining motivation, building momentum, and ultimately achieving lasting success. It reinforces positive behaviors, fosters a sense of accomplishment, and fuels the drive to continue striving for greatness.

Celebrating success is not merely about indulging in fleeting moments of joy; it is a deliberate practice that can have a profound impact on our overall well-being and performance. When we take the time to acknowledge our accomplishments, we reinforce the neural pathways associated with positive emotions and behaviors. This, in turn, strengthens our motivation and makes it more likely that we will repeat those successful actions in the future.

Furthermore, celebrating success helps to cultivate a positive mindset. It shifts our focus from what we haven't achieved to what we have, fostering gratitude and appreciation for our efforts. This positive outlook can be contagious, inspiring others around us and creating a more supportive and encouraging environment. When we celebrate our successes together, we build a collective sense of accomplishment that can propel us towards even greater achievements.

Recognizing achievements is not just about external validation or material rewards. It is also about internal recognition, acknowledging the effort,
dedication, and resilience that went into achieving a goal. This internal recognition can be just as powerful, if not more so, than external praise. It reinforces our self-belief, boosts our confidence, and reminds us of our capabilities. When we internalize our successes, we develop a strong sense of self-efficacy, which is the belief in our ability to succeed. This belief can be a powerful motivator, fueling our drive to take on new challenges and pursue our dreams.

Building momentum is another key benefit of celebrating success. When we acknowledge our achievements, we create a sense of progress and forward movement. This can be particularly important when facing setbacks or challenges. By focusing on our wins, we remind ourselves of our capabilities and resilience, which can help us to bounce back from adversity and keep moving forward. Celebrating small wins along the way can also help to maintain motivation and prevent burnout. It reminds us that we are making progress, even if the ultimate goal seems far off.

Celebrating success can take many forms. It could be as simple as taking a moment to reflect on your accomplishments, sharing your wins with friends or colleagues, or treating yourself to something special. It could also involve setting new goals, taking on new challenges, or simply basking in the glow of your achievements. The key is to find what works for you and make celebrating success a regular part of your routine.

It's also important to celebrate the successes of others. By acknowledging and appreciating the achievements of our colleagues, friends, and family members, we create a culture of support and encouragement. This can foster a sense of camaraderie and shared purpose, which can be a powerful motivator for everyone involved. Celebrating the successes of others also helps to build stronger relationships and create a more positive and supportive environment.

In conclusion, celebrating success is not just a feel-good exercise; it is a powerful tool for personal and professional growth. By recognizing and appreciating our achievements, both big and small, we reinforce positive behaviors, cultivate a positive mindset, and build momentum towards our goals. It is a practice that can empower us to overcome challenges, achieve lasting success, and create a more fulfilling life. So, take the time to celebrate your wins, acknowledge your efforts, and appreciate the journey. Remember, success is not just about reaching the destination; it's about enjoying the ride along the way.

ᐧᐧᐧ

Celebrating success is not just about indulging in self-praise; it's about acknowledging your hard work, recognizing your achievements, and fueling your motivation for future endeavors. Remember, every win, no matter how small, deserves to be celebrated.

FIFTEEN

Paying it Forward: Supporting the Next Generation of Women Leaders

The journey of women's empowerment is a continuous one, a relay race where the baton of knowledge, experience, and opportunity is passed from one generation to the next. The concept of "paying it forward" embodies this spirit of intergenerational support, where women who have achieved success use their position to uplift and empower the next generation of women leaders. It is a virtuous cycle of mentorship, sponsorship, and advocacy that creates a ripple effect of positive change, transforming the landscape for women in all spheres of life.

Paying it forward is not simply about altruism; it is a strategic investment in the future. By supporting the next generation of women leaders, we are creating a pipeline of talent that will drive innovation, solve complex problems, and lead us towards a more equitable and just society. We are also ensuring that the progress we have made towards gender equality is not only sustained but accelerated. When women lift each other up, we create a collective force that is unstoppable.

Mentorship is a cornerstone of paying it forward. By sharing their knowledge, experience, and insights, mentors can provide invaluable guidance and support to young women who are just starting their careers. A mentor can offer a listening ear, a sounding board for ideas, and a safe space to explore challenges and opportunities. They can also provide access to networks and resources that can open doors and accelerate career growth. Mentorship is not just about giving advice; it is about fostering a relationship of trust, respect, and mutual learning.

Sponsorship is another powerful way to pay it forward. While mentorship focuses on personal and professional development, sponsorship involves actively advocating for and promoting the advancement of a promising individual. Sponsors use their influence and connections to open doors, create opportunities, and ensure that their protégés are recognized and rewarded for their contributions. By actively sponsoring women, we can help to break down barriers and create a more level playing field.

Advocacy is another crucial aspect of paying it forward. It involves speaking out against injustice, challenging discriminatory practices, and promoting policies that support women's rights and advancement. Women who have achieved success have a unique platform to amplify their voices and advocate for change. By using their influence to champion women's issues, they can create a ripple effect that inspires others to take action and create a more equitable world.

Paying it forward is not just about individual actions; it is also about creating a culture of support and empowerment. This involves fostering a workplace environment where women feel valued and respected, where their contributions are recognized, and where they have equal opportunities for advancement. It also means challenging stereotypes and biases, both conscious and unconscious, that can hold women back. By creating a more inclusive and supportive culture, we can unlock the full potential of women and create a more prosperous and equitable society.

In the digital age, technology has opened up new avenues for paying it forward. Online mentorship platforms, virtual networking events, and social media groups provide accessible and convenient ways to connect with and support young women leaders. By leveraging these tools, women can expand their reach and impact, creating a global network of support and empowerment.

The benefits of paying it forward are not just limited to the mentee or protégé; they also extend to the mentor or sponsor. By giving back to their community, mentors and sponsors can gain a sense of purpose, fulfillment, and renewed passion for their work. They can also learn from the fresh perspectives and insights of their mentees, which can help them to stay relevant and adaptable in a rapidly changing world.

In conclusion, paying it forward is a powerful way to empower the next generation of women leaders and create a more equitable and just society. It is a continuous cycle of mentorship, sponsorship, and advocacy that creates a ripple effect of positive change. By investing in the development of young women, we are not only helping them to achieve their dreams but also building a brighter future for all. Let us all commit to paying it forward, to lifting each other up, and to creating a world where all women have the opportunity to thrive.

ᗡᗡᗡ

Paying it forward is not just a moral obligation; it's a strategic investment in the future. By supporting the next generation of women leaders, we are ensuring that the progress we have made towards gender equality continues. Remember, empowered women empower women.

SIXTEEN

BUILDING A LEGACY: THE LASTING IMPACT OF STRATEGIC ALLIANCES

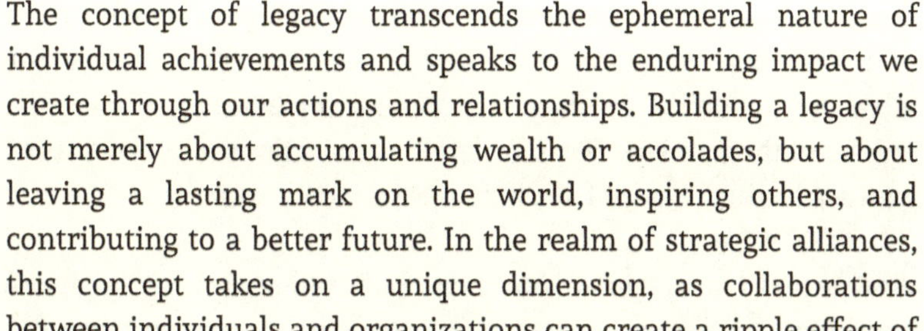

The concept of legacy transcends the ephemeral nature of individual achievements and speaks to the enduring impact we create through our actions and relationships. Building a legacy is not merely about accumulating wealth or accolades, but about leaving a lasting mark on the world, inspiring others, and contributing to a better future. In the realm of strategic alliances, this concept takes on a unique dimension, as collaborations between individuals and organizations can create a ripple effect of positive change that extends far beyond the immediate goals of the alliance.

Strategic alliances, when thoughtfully crafted and nurtured, have the potential to create a legacy that outlives the individuals and organizations involved. These collaborations can leave an enduring impact on industries, communities, and even society as a whole. By aligning their visions, resources, and expertise, partners in a strategic alliance can achieve outcomes that would be impossible to attain individually. This shared success not only benefits the partners themselves but also creates a ripple effect of positive change that can benefit countless others.

One of the most significant ways strategic alliances can build a lasting legacy is through innovation and the creation of new knowledge. By combining their unique perspectives, skills, and resources, partners can develop groundbreaking solutions to complex problems, push the boundaries of their respective fields, and create new products, services, or technologies that have a lasting impact on society. These innovations can transform industries, improve lives, and leave a lasting mark on the world.

Strategic alliances can also build a legacy through their impact on communities and social causes. By partnering with organizations that share their values and commitment to social responsibility, businesses can create alliances that address critical social issues, empower marginalized communities, and promote sustainable development. These alliances can fund research, provide education and training, support community development projects, or advocate for policy changes that benefit society as a whole. The impact of these alliances can be felt for generations to come, as they create a lasting legacy of social impact.

Another way strategic alliances can build a legacy is through the development of human capital. By investing in the growth and development of their employees, partners can create a highly skilled and motivated workforce that is capable of achieving great things. This can involve providing training and development opportunities, mentoring and coaching programs, and creating a culture of learning and innovation. By empowering their employees to reach their full potential, organizations can build a legacy of talent that will continue to drive innovation and success long after the alliance has ended.

Strategic alliances can also create a legacy through their impact on the environment. By partnering with organizations committed to sustainability, businesses can develop and implement environmentally friendly practices that reduce their carbon footprint, conserve resources, and protect the planet. These alliances can also fund research into new technologies and solutions that address environmental challenges. By taking a proactive approach to environmental sustainability, businesses can build a legacy of responsible stewardship that will benefit future generations.

Building a legacy through strategic alliances requires a long-term perspective and a commitment to shared values. It is not simply about achieving short-term gains, but about creating lasting value for all stakeholders involved. This requires a willingness to invest in relationships, build trust, and work collaboratively towards a common vision. It also requires a commitment to continuous improvement, innovation, and social responsibility.

In conclusion, strategic alliances have the power to build a lasting legacy that extends far beyond the immediate goals of the partnership. By focusing on innovation, social impact, human capital development, and environmental sustainability, alliances can create a ripple effect of positive change that benefits individuals, organizations, communities, and the planet. By embracing a long-term perspective and a commitment to shared values, we can build a legacy that will inspire and empower future generations.

ᗐᗐᗐ

Building a legacy is not just about leaving a mark on the world; it's about creating a ripple effect of positive change that inspires others and transforms lives. Strategic alliances, when built on shared values and a commitment to social impact, can create a legacy that lasts for generations.

SEVENTEEN

Thriving Together: The Power of Collective Action

In the tapestry of human existence, the threads of individual lives are inextricably woven together. Our collective well-being and progress depend not only on our individual efforts but also on our ability to collaborate, cooperate, and take collective action.

This fundamental truth applies to all facets of life, from social movements and political activism to business ventures and personal relationships. The power of collective action lies in its ability to amplify individual voices, pool resources, and create a shared sense of purpose that drives transformative change.

At its core, collective action is about recognizing that we are stronger together than we are alone. When individuals unite around a common goal, they create a force that is greater than the sum of its parts. This collective power can be harnessed to achieve outcomes that would be impossible for individuals to achieve on their own.

Whether it's advocating for social justice, tackling environmental challenges, or building a thriving community, collective action can create a ripple effect of positive change that extends far beyond the immediate participants.

One of the most powerful aspects of collective action is its ability to amplify individual voices. When people come together to speak out against injustice, demand change, or advocate for their rights, their voices become a chorus that cannot be ignored.

This collective voice can influence public opinion, pressure decision-makers, and ultimately lead to policy changes that benefit society as a whole. Throughout history, social movements have demonstrated the transformative power of collective action, from the civil rights movement to the fight for women's suffrage to the environmental movement.

Collective action also enables the pooling of resources, which can be essential for achieving complex goals. When individuals contribute their time, money, skills, and expertise, they create a collective pool of resources that can be used to fund research, provide services, launch campaigns, or build infrastructure. This pooling of resources can be particularly impactful for marginalized communities, who may lack the individual resources to address their needs and advocate for their rights. By coming together, these communities can leverage their collective power to create meaningful change.

Furthermore, collective action fosters a sense of community and belonging. When people work together towards a common goal, they develop a shared sense of purpose and identity. This shared purpose can transcend individual differences and create a sense of solidarity that binds people together.

This sense of community can be a powerful source of support, motivation, and resilience, especially in the face of adversity. It can also create a sense of hope and optimism, as individuals see that their actions can make a real difference in the world.

In the business world, collective action can take the form of collaborations, partnerships, and industry-wide initiatives. By working together, businesses can share knowledge, pool resources, and develop innovative solutions to common challenges.

This can lead to increased efficiency, reduced costs, and improved competitiveness. Collaborative efforts can also help to address social and environmental issues, such as climate change, labor rights, and responsible sourcing.

In the realm of personal relationships, collective action can manifest as mutual support, shared decision-making, and collaborative problem-solving. When individuals come together to support each other through difficult times, celebrate achievements, and work together to overcome challenges, they create stronger bonds and more fulfilling relationships.

This sense of collective responsibility and shared purpose can also extend to families, communities, and society as a whole.

However, collective action is not without its challenges. Building consensus, coordinating efforts, and managing conflict can be difficult. It requires effective communication, leadership, and a willingness to compromise. It also requires a shared understanding of the goals and values that underpin the collective action.

Despite these challenges, the power of collective action is undeniable. By working together, we can achieve more than we ever could alone. Whether it's advocating for social justice, tackling environmental challenges, building a thriving business, or strengthening our personal relationships, collective action has the power to transform our lives and create a better world for all.

ᐅᐅᐅ

Thriving together is not just a utopian ideal; it's a practical necessity. By embracing the power of collective action, we can overcome challenges, achieve our goals, and create a more equitable and sustainable world. Remember, our individual well-being is inextricably linked to the well-being of our communities and the planet.

EIGHTEEN

Networking for Social Impact: Creating Change Through Connection

In an era marked by interconnectedness and a growing awareness of social responsibility, the traditional concept of networking is evolving into a powerful tool for creating positive change. Networking for social impact goes beyond the exchange of business cards and superficial connections; it is a deliberate and intentional approach to building relationships that drive social change. By leveraging the power of connection, individuals and organizations can create a ripple effect of positive impact that extends far beyond their immediate circles.

At its core, networking for social impact is about building relationships with a purpose. It involves identifying individuals and organizations that share a common vision for a better world and working together to achieve that vision. This can involve connecting with like-minded individuals, forming partnerships with organizations that share your values, and leveraging your network to amplify the impact of social initiatives. By approaching networking with a focus on social impact, you can create a powerful network of change-makers who are committed to making a difference in the world.

One of the key benefits of networking for social impact is the ability to access and mobilize resources. Social change often requires a significant investment of time, money, and expertise. By building a strong network of individuals and organizations committed to social impact, you can tap into a vast pool of resources that can help you achieve your goals. This can include funding for projects, access to expertise and knowledge, and support for advocacy and outreach efforts. By leveraging the collective power of your network, you can amplify your impact and achieve results that would be impossible to achieve alone.

Another important aspect of networking for social impact is the ability to build coalitions and partnerships. Social change rarely happens in isolation. It requires collaboration and cooperation across different sectors and stakeholders. By building relationships with individuals and organizations from diverse backgrounds, you can create powerful coalitions that can advocate for change, influence policy, and drive social innovation. These partnerships can also help to bridge divides, build trust, and create a shared sense of purpose that can lead to lasting change.

Networking for social impact also involves sharing knowledge and expertise. By connecting with experts and thought leaders in your field, you can gain valuable insights, learn from their experiences, and stay abreast of the latest developments in social impact. This knowledge can be used to inform your own work, develop innovative solutions to social problems, and inspire others to take action. By sharing your own knowledge and expertise with others, you can also contribute to a collective pool of knowledge that can drive social change.

In the digital age, technology has opened up new avenues for networking for social impact. Social media platforms, online communities, and virtual events provide accessible and convenient ways to connect with people from all over the world who share your passion for social change. By leveraging these tools, you can build a global network of change-makers, share ideas and resources, and collaborate on projects that have a global impact.

However, networking for social impact is not just about online interactions. Building strong and meaningful relationships often requires face-to-face interactions, where you can build trust, establish rapport, and develop a deeper understanding of each other's perspectives and goals. By attending conferences, workshops, and other events focused on social impact, you can connect with like-minded individuals, learn from experts, and build relationships that can lead to lasting change.

It's also important to remember that networking for social impact is not just about what you can get from others, but also about what you can give. By volunteering your time, skills, and resources to social causes, you can make a direct impact on the lives of others and contribute to a better world. Volunteering can also be a great way to meet other people who share your passion for social change and build relationships that can lead to further collaboration.

In conclusion, networking for social impact is a powerful tool for creating positive change. By building relationships with a purpose, accessing and mobilizing resources, building coalitions and partnerships, sharing knowledge and expertise, and leveraging technology, individuals and organizations can create a ripple effect of positive impact that extends far beyond their immediate circles.

By embracing the power of connection, we can create a more just, equitable, and sustainable world for all.

ⱣⱣⱣ

Networking for social impact is not just about making connections; it's about using your network to create positive change. Connect with like-minded individuals, collaborate on projects that matter, and amplify the voices of those who are marginalized. Remember, even small actions can have a big impact when we work together.

NINETEEN

CULTIVATING CONFIDENCE: STEPPING INTO YOUR POWER AS A NETWORKER"

In the dynamic arena of networking, confidence is not merely an asset; it's a driving force that propels individuals towards success. It's the inner strength that allows you to approach new people, initiate conversations, and forge meaningful connections. For women, who may face unique challenges and societal expectations, cultivating confidence is essential for stepping into their power as networkers and achieving their full potential.

Confidence is not about arrogance or self-aggrandizement. It is a quiet assurance in one's abilities, a belief in one's worth, and a willingness to put oneself out there. It is the foundation upon which successful networking is built. A confident networker exudes an aura of positivity and approachability, making others feel comfortable and eager to engage. This, in turn, opens doors to new opportunities, collaborations, and relationships.

Building confidence as a networker is a journey that requires self-reflection, intentional practice, and a willingness to step outside one's comfort zone. It begins with recognizing your strengths and acknowledging your unique value proposition. What skills, experiences, and perspectives do you bring to the table? What makes you stand out from the crowd? By identifying and embracing your strengths, you can build a solid foundation of self-belief that will radiate in your interactions with others.

Preparation is key to cultivating confidence. Before attending a networking event or meeting, take the time to research the attendees, the organization, and the industry. This will equip you with talking points and help you to feel more knowledgeable and engaged. Practice your elevator pitch, prepare a few questions to ask others, and visualize yourself having successful conversations. The more prepared you are, the more confident you will feel.

Networking can be intimidating, but it's important to remember that everyone feels nervous at times. The key is to not let fear hold you back. Challenge yourself to step outside your comfort zone, approach new people, and initiate conversations. Remember, the worst that can happen is that someone says no or is not interested. The more you practice, the easier it will become.

One of the most effective ways to build confidence is to focus on building relationships rather than collecting business cards. Approach networking as an opportunity to connect with others on a human level. Ask questions, listen actively, and show genuine interest in their stories and experiences. By focusing on building authentic connections, you will not only feel more confident but also create more meaningful and lasting relationships.

Another way to boost your confidence is to celebrate your successes. When you achieve a networking goal, whether it's landing a new client, securing a speaking engagement, or simply having a great conversation, take the time to acknowledge and celebrate your accomplishment. This will reinforce positive behaviors and build momentum for future success.

Mentorship can also play a crucial role in cultivating confidence. A mentor can offer guidance, support, and encouragement as you navigate the challenges of networking. They can also provide valuable feedback and help you to identify areas for growth. By seeking out mentors who inspire and empower you, you can accelerate your development as a networker and build the confidence needed to achieve your goals.

It's important to remember that confidence is not a fixed trait; it is a skill that can be developed and strengthened over time. By practicing self-reflection, preparation, and intentional action, you can overcome self-doubt, embrace your strengths, and step into your power as a networker. Remember, you have unique gifts and talents to offer the world. By sharing your expertise, insights, and passion with others, you can make a meaningful impact and create a fulfilling and successful career.

In conclusion, cultivating confidence is a journey of self-discovery, growth, and empowerment. By embracing your strengths, challenging your fears, and building authentic connections, you can become a confident and impactful networker. Remember, your voice matters, your ideas are valuable, and your presence is a gift. Step into your power, embrace your unique voice, and make your mark on the world.

ᐅᐅᐅ

Confidence is not a personality trait; it's a skill that can be cultivated. Believe in your abilities, embrace your unique voice, and step outside your comfort zone. Remember, your confidence is contagious, and it can inspire others to do the same.

TWENTY

The Ripple Effect: Transforming Your Life and Career Through Networking

Networking, often perceived as a transactional exchange of business cards or a means to an end, has a profound and transformative power that extends far beyond its surface-level interactions. It is a catalyst for personal and professional growth, a vehicle for creating opportunities, and a force that can ripple through our lives, leaving a lasting impact on our careers and overall well-being.

At its core, networking is about building relationships. It's about connecting with others on a human level, sharing experiences, exchanging ideas, and supporting each other's aspirations. These connections, when nurtured and cultivated, can have a ripple effect that extends far beyond the initial interaction. A single conversation can spark a new idea, a chance encounter can lead to a dream job, and a supportive relationship can provide the encouragement needed to overcome challenges and achieve success.

The ripple effect of networking begins with the individual. When we connect with others, we expand our knowledge, gain new perspectives, and challenge our assumptions. We learn from the experiences of others, discover new opportunities, and broaden our horizons. This personal growth and development can lead to increased confidence, improved communication skills, and a greater sense of purpose. By investing in our networks, we are investing in ourselves, and the benefits can be both immediate and long-lasting.

As we grow and evolve through our network connections, our careers also begin to transform. Networking opens doors to new opportunities, whether it's a job referral, a speaking engagement, or a chance to collaborate on a project. It can also provide access to mentors and sponsors who can offer guidance, support, and advocacy. By tapping into the collective wisdom and resources of our network, we can accelerate our career growth, achieve our goals, and make a meaningful impact in our chosen field.

The ripple effect of networking extends beyond our individual careers. As we connect with others, we become part of a larger community. We share our knowledge and expertise, support each other's endeavors, and celebrate each other's successes. This sense of community can be a powerful source of support, motivation, and inspiration. It can also lead to collaborations and partnerships that create a greater impact than any individual could achieve alone.

Networking can also have a profound impact on our personal lives. The relationships we build through networking can provide emotional support, encouragement, and a sense of belonging. They can also introduce us to new hobbies, interests, and experiences that enrich our lives. By connecting with people from diverse backgrounds and perspectives, we can broaden our horizons, challenge our assumptions, and develop a deeper understanding of the world around us.

The ripple effect of networking is not limited to the present; it can also extend to future generations. By mentoring and supporting young professionals, we can help them to develop the skills, knowledge, and connections they need to succeed. We can also inspire them to pursue their passions, make a difference in the world, and create their own ripple effects of positive change.

In conclusion, networking is a powerful force that can transform our lives and careers. It is not just about exchanging business cards or attending social events; it is about building meaningful relationships, sharing knowledge, and supporting each other's aspirations. The ripple effect of networking is a testament to the interconnectedness of our lives and the power of human connection. By investing in our networks, we are investing in ourselves, our communities, and the future.

ppp

The ripple effect of networking is a testament to the interconnectedness of our lives. By building meaningful relationships, supporting each other's aspirations, and sharing our knowledge and resources, we can create a ripple effect of positive change that transforms our lives, our careers, and the world around us.

TWENTY-ONE
SUMMARY

The power of networking and connectedness for women cannot be overstated. Beyond the traditional exchange of business cards, it's about fostering genuine, meaningful relationships that empower women to achieve their full potential. By redefining networking and building strategic alliances, women unlock a world of opportunities for personal and professional growth.

Redefining Networking for Women

Networking is more than just collecting contacts; it's about cultivating authentic relationships based on trust, mutual respect, and shared values. Women thrive in collaborative environments, where mentorship and a sense of belonging are fostered. By shifting the focus from quantity to quality, women can build a network of meaningful connections that provide lasting support and guidance.

Unlocking the Potential of Women's Networks

Women's networks are a powerful force for change. These intentional communities provide a safe space for women to connect, share experiences, and learn from one another. Through the exchange of knowledge, advocacy, and mentorship, women's networks empower individuals to overcome challenges, develop leadership skills, and advance their careers. These networks also have a broader impact, driving social change and creating a more equitable world.

Creating Strategic Alliances for Mutual Success

Strategic alliances are dynamic relationships built on trust and shared vision. By leveraging complementary strengths and resources, women can achieve goals that would be unattainable alone. These alliances provide access to new markets, expand knowledge, and foster a sense of community. Successful alliances require careful planning, open communication, and a commitment to mutual benefit.

Navigating the Landscape for Women in Networking and Leadership

Women face unique challenges in the world of networking and leadership, including gender stereotypes and unconscious biases. By understanding these challenges and developing effective strategies, women can navigate this landscape with confidence. Building strong networks, seeking out mentors and sponsors, and embracing their unique leadership styles are all key components of success. Technology has also opened up new avenues for women to connect and collaborate, creating a more inclusive and supportive environment.

Cultivating Authenticity in Professional Relationships

Authenticity is the cornerstone of meaningful professional relationships. By being true to themselves, women can attract like-minded individuals who appreciate their genuine approach. Building authentic connections involves self-awareness, active listening, open communication, and a willingness to be vulnerable. These connections can lead to increased trust, collaboration, and job satisfaction, ultimately contributing to a more fulfilling and successful career.

Mastering the Art of Conversation for Effective Networking

Effective networking conversations require more than just small talk. They involve active listening, thoughtful questions, and the ability to articulate one's own ideas and experiences in a compelling way. Nonverbal communication, such as body language and tone of voice, also plays a crucial role in building rapport. By mastering the art of conversation, women can create lasting impressions, expand their professional circles, and unlock a world of opportunities.

Empowering Women Through Mentorship and Support

Mentorship is a transformative force for women, providing guidance, support, and access to networks and opportunities. A mentor can share their expertise, offer encouragement, and help women to navigate challenges and achieve their goals. Conversely, becoming a mentor allows women to give back to their community and empower the next generation of leaders. By fostering a culture of mentorship, we can create a powerful network of women who lift each other up and achieve collective success.

The Ripple Effect of Networking

Networking has a ripple effect that extends far beyond the initial connection. It can lead to personal growth, career advancement, and positive social impact. By building strong relationships, sharing knowledge, and supporting each other's aspirations, women can create a ripple effect of positive change that transforms their lives, their communities, and the world.

In conclusion, the power of networking and connectedness is undeniable. By embracing authenticity, building strategic alliances, and supporting each other, women can break down barriers, overcome challenges, and achieve unprecedented success. The ripple effect of these connections will not only transform individual lives and careers but also contribute to a more equitable, inclusive, and prosperous future for all.

ፆፆፆ

Citation And References

This book represents the culmination of extensive research and meticulous analysis, incorporating a diverse range of sources, including numerous books, scholarly studies, and personal experiences. Additionally, I have scoured various websites to gather relevant information and data essential for the compilation of this work. I have taken every precaution to ensure the accuracy of the information presented and have diligently cited all sources to acknowledge their contributions.

Despite these efforts, the possibility of inadvertent errors remains. I deeply value the insights of my readers and appreciate any feedback that can help identify and rectify such inaccuracies. I encourage you to bring any discrepancies to my attention.

Your feedback is not only welcome but crucial, as it will aid in correcting current editions and enhancing the content of future ones. I am committed to maintaining the highest standards of accuracy and reliability in my work and thank you for your support and understanding.

Additionally, I firmly uphold the principle of freedom of speech and expression as guaranteed under Article 19(1)(a) of the Constitution of India, and I respect the diverse viewpoints and expressions of all readers.

ৼৼৼ

Other Books Of The Author

1. Empowering Minds: A Journey into Women's Self-Discovery and Power
2. The Dynamics of Motivation: Catalyzing Thought into Action
3. Meditation and Mental Well Being: The Path to Inner Peace and Clarity
4. The Psychology of Child Education: Nurturing Future Generations
5. Ethical Enlightenment: A Modern Guide to Living with Integrity
6. Voices of Empowerment: Stories of Women Rising Against Odds
7. Social Psychology in Everyday Life: Understanding Human Connections
8. The Essence of Motivational Speaking: Inspiring Change in Others
9. Balancing Acts: Women, Work, and the Will to Lead
10. Guiding with Grace: Raising Children with Compassion and Awareness
11. The Power of Positive Aging: Embracing Life After Fifty
12. Building Resilient Communities: Social Work in Action
13. The Ethical Educator: Principles for Teaching and Learning
14. From Insight to Impact: Social Psychology for a Better World
15. The Ethics of Empathy: A Guide to Ethical Living
16. The Science of Empowering the Self: Navigating Life's Challenges with Psychological Wisdom
17. The Mindful Conscious Leader: Meditation Techniques for Modern Management
18. Pioneering Spirit: Women's Pathways to Leadership and Empowerment
19. Feeling to Healing: The Role of Emotional Intelligence in Child Development
20. Transformative Talks and Words of Inspiration: Insights into Motivational Oratory

21. Green Ethics: A Path to Sustainable Living
22. Spiritual Integrity: Navigating Life with Moral Compassion
23. Clean Living, Clean Society: The Ethics of Cleanliness
24. Patriotic Spirits: Building a Nation on Positive Attitudes
25. Innovative Integrity & Vibrant Visions: The Ethical and Entrepreneurial Spirit of Gujarat
26. Youthful Visions, Endless Possibilities: Inspiring Ethics and Motivation in Children
27. Living Your Legacy: How to Motivate Others by Living Your Values
28. Secret of Healing Conversations: Ethical Practices in Counselling and Therapy
29. Creative Kindness: Crafting a Life of Compassion and Creativity
30. The Power of Appreciation: How Gratitude Can Transform Your Relationships
31. Bhagavad-Gita: Messages
32. Science of Art: The New Frontier of Fashion Modernism
33. Vivekananda's Virtues: A Blueprint for Modern Living
34. Empower Her: Navigating the Path to Women's Entrepreneurship
35. The Boundless Classroom: Innovations in Global Education
36. The Language of Leadership: Communicating with Authenticity and Impact
37. The Warrior's Mantra: Deciphering the Hanuman Chalisa
38. Echoes of Empathy: Transformative Stories of Social Service
39. Artful Living: Cultivating Creativity in Your Daily Routine
40. Finding Your Why: Discovering Your Passions and Charting Your Course
41. The Role of Social Media in Shaping Self-Esteem and Interpersonal Relationships among Adolescents
42. Karma's Tapestry: Weaving a Life of Selfless Service
43. Altruistic Alchemy: Transforming Lives Through Giving
44. The Blueprint of Pro-Activeness and Productivity: Crafting Habits for Success
45. The Simplicity with Grounded Wisdom: Embracing Authenticity

in a Complex World

46. Secret of Solopreneur's Odyssey: Navigating the Path to Self-Employment
47. Exploring Tapestry of Peace: Global Perspectives on Harmony
48. The Art and Actions of Connection: Mastering Communication for Impact
49. She Governs and at the Helm: Strategies for Political Empowerment
50. Rising Above and Rising with Grace: A Woman's Roadmap to Career Mastery
51. The Effect of Networking & Connectedness: Building Strategic Alliances for Women
52. Beyond his Barriers: Women Thriving in Male-Dominated Fields
53. Secret of Inner Compass: Navigating Life with Intuition
54. Creative & Pro-Active Muses: A Celebration of Women in the Arts
55. Unburdened: The Art of Releasing the Past
56. Amplified Voices: Speeches of Women that Astonished the World
57. Secret of Manifesting Dreams: A Woman's Guide to Intentional Living
58. Ethics and Value Based Education: Reimagining Japan's School System
59. The Moral Compass Curriculum: A Holistic Approach
60. Tech with Heart: Integrating Ethics into Digital Learning
61. Honoring Virtue: Recognizing Ethical Excellence in Education
62. Raising Good Humans: A Guide to Character Development
63. The Spark Within: Nurturing Creativity in Children
64. The Teenager Whisperer: Navigating Adolescence with Grace
65. Igniting a Passion for Learning: Inspiring Lifelong Curiosity
66. The Habit Lab: Cultivating Positive Behaviors in Children
67. Seeds of Empathy: Fostering Compassion in Young Hearts
68. The Reading Revolution: Inspiring a Love of Books in Children
69. The Learning Brain: Unlocking the Secrets of Student Success
70. Teaching for All: Differentiated Instruction Strategies
71. The Time Alchemist: Mastering Time Management for Peak Performance

72. The Resilience Factor: Transforming Setbacks into Stepping Stones
73. The Healing Touch of Nature: An Introduction to Naturopathy
74. Echoes of the Past: Healing Through Past Life Regression
75. The Spiritual Healer's Handbook: Exploring Energy Medicine
76. Crystal Clarity: Unveiling the Power of Gemstones
77. The Dream Weaver's Guide: Decoding the Language of Dreams
78. Emotional Alchemy: Transforming Pain into Power
79. Sonic Serenity: Harnessing Sound for Stress Relief
80. The Entrepreneur's Playbook: Launching Your Business with Confidence
81. Productivity Unleashed: Time Management Strategies for Entrepreneurs
82. The Problem Solver's Toolkit: Creative Solutions for Business Challenges
83. The Future is Now: Emerging Trends in Business
84. The Curious Explorer: A Child's Guide to Scientific Discovery
85. Digital Pioneers: Empowering Kids in the Tech World
86. The Young Philosopher's Guide: Exploring Life's Big Questions
87. Finding Your Voice: Communication Skills for Confident Kids
88. Nature's Playground: A Child's Guide to Outdoor Adventure
89. Growing a Greener Tomorrow: A Guide to Tree Planting & Conservation
90. Driving with Purpose: Ethical Choices on the Road
91. The Healing Touch: Cultivating Compassion in Healthcare
92. Navigating the Digital Landscape: Ethics in the Age of Social Media
93. The Ethical Closet: A Guide to Sustainable Fashion
94. The Mindful Voyager: Sustainable Travel Practices
95. The Feminine Divine: Honoring the Goddesses of India
96. Sacred Sounds: Chanting Your Way to Inner Peace
97. The Yoga Path: Uniting with the Divine Within
98. Rites of Passage: Creating Meaningful Ceremonies
99. The Chakra System: A Map of Inner Transformation
100. Spiritual Sangha: Finding Community through Satsang and

Bhajan
101. Pilgrimage of the Soul: Spiritual Journeys in India

❧❧❧

• 131 •

Bhajan
101. Pilgrimage of the Soul: Spiritual Journeys in India

❧❧❧

Contact

Dr. Minakshi Bansal
Social Activist
Ahmedabad, Gujarat, Bharat
minakshiindiag20@yahoo.com

❥❥❥

|| LOKAHA SAMASTHAHA SUKHINO BHAVANTU ||